How Can I Be Sure?

A PRE-MARRIAGE INVENTORY

Including: A sample wedding
ceremony and a wedding checklist

Bob Phillips

D1399931

Harvest House Publishers
Irvine, California 92714

AKNOWLEDGMENTS

I would like to extend a personal word of thanks to the following individuals who took time out of their busy schedules to read this manuscript and make comments and suggestions:

DR. VINCE BLOOM, Associate Professor of Speech Communications at California State University, Fresno

DR. HENRY BRANDT, Counseling Psychologist

DR. RAY BREWER, Professor of Education at California State University, Fresno

RICHARD DICKSON, Professor of Psychology at El Camino College and Licensed Marriage, Family and Child Counselor

DR. HOWARD HENDRICKS, Chairman of the Dept. of Christian Education, Dallas Theological Seminary

REV. BUFE KARRAKER, Pastor of Northwest Church, Fresno and Executive Director of Fresno Youth for Christ

DR. TIM LA HAYE, Pastor of Scott Memorial Church, San Diego; President of Christian Heritage College; Director of Family Life Seminars; and author of numerous books

DR. JEANNE O'DELL, Clinical Psychologist and Licensed Marriage, Family and Child Counselor

KEN POURE, Extension Director for Hume Lake Christian Camps and Director of Accent Crusades, Inc.

DR. EARL RADMACHER, President of Western Baptist Seminary, Portland, Oregon

DR. RAY STEDMAN, Pastor of the Peninsula Bible Church, Palo Alto and author of numerous books

DR. JAY STEVANS, Associate Pastor of Northwest Church, Fresno

DR. PAUL SUNDSTROM, Professor of Pastoral Psychology, Western Baptist Seminary, Portland, Oregon

REV. RICK YOHN, Pastor of Evangelical Free Church of Fresno, California and author of numerous books

About the Author

- Associate Pastor of Counseling Ministries at Northwest Church, Fresno, California

- Former Assistant Director of Hume Lake Christian Camps

- Graduate of Biola College, La Mirada, California

- Graduate of California State University, Fresno with a Masters in Counseling

- Licensed Marriage, Family, and Child Counselor

- Author of ten books totaling over one half million copies in print

- Popular speaker in family life seminars, churches, and conferences

- Devoted Christian husband and father of two children, and believes that his family ranks at the top of his system of priorities and values

WHAT DR. HOWARD HENDRICKS
SAYS ABOUT THIS BOOK

Premarital counseling can make the difference between a successful and unsuccessful marriage. HOW CAN I BE SURE is a resourceful aid for evaluating and enhancing a good and lasting marital relationship. Couples without the benefit of premarital counseling will find it an excellent communication prompter.

HOW CAN I BE SURE

Copyright © 1978, Harvest House Publishers
Irvine, CA 92714

Library of Congress Catalog Card Number 77-94448
ISBN 0-89081-073-7

Printed in the United States of America.

Dedicated to

KEN POURE

—Man of God

—Leader of men

—Spiritual father
in the faith

—My best friend

Contents

Introduction

I hurt!

No, I'm not feeling any physical pain, I hurt emotionally. My pain comes from the anguish and suffering I have shared listening to couples relate to me the despair, frustration and sense of hopelessness they are experiencing in their marriages.

I am a counselor, so my job is to listen and to help. But I do more than listen, I suffer with these couples. Part of my anguish comes from the realization that many of the problems I hear could have been avoided. So many times I have thought to myself—"If only I could have counseled with this couple before they were married."

As a busy counseling pastor, I found that I was not only becoming involved with more and more divorce cases, but also with more and more premarital counseling. As I became involved in premarital counseling, I discovered a different type of frustration. How many sessions should I spend with a couple? What material should we cover? How much is enough? How can we approach sensitive subjects?

Jonathan Swift said, "Necessity is the mother of invention." The need for tools to help build strong foundations for marriage coupled with my frustration in premarital counseling led to the creation of this premarriage inventory.

This inventory is not an answer book for marriage problems. Many of these types of books have already been written and are available. This inventory is a discussion guide to help couples open up important channels of communication, express their thoughts, desires and feelings to each other, and enhance their growing relationship together.

Each person should have a personal copy in which to write his or her own responses. If you will honestly share with each other your thoughts and feelings with regard to the questions, your future marriage will begin on a strong, firm and mutually satisfying foundation.

Married couples can also benefit from a review of the questions. Discussing your responses together will help to open up new channels of communication, and will also help clarify any misunderstandings that may exist. Your love for each other will be revived, restored and reinforced.

It is my prayer that you will find help and encouragement in these pages for your marriage and that God will be glorified as a result.

Bob Phillips
Fresno, California

Ways to Use This Book

This book is designed to be a helpful tool in the hands of a pastor or counselor. Therefore, you may want to present copies to the couple or have both parties purchase their own copy.

In premarital counseling, it will be helpful to have the couple fill out the first three chapters prior to the initial session. A lot of time can be lost in counseling when either party or both have not considered certain topics ahead of time. This is complicated even further if the couple is embarrassed with the presentation of material that they have not yet discussed together. This is especially true in the area of sexual or financial topics.

Many couples have no idea what is involved in premarital counseling. This inventory helps to eliminate some of the fear and frustration and will greatly enhance the quality of the counseling sessions. The inventory will also help to add consistency to the pastor or counselors premarital counseling program. The couples should be encouraged to complete the various homework assignments and bring the inventory with them to each session.

In developing this inventory, I have suggested six counseling sessions prior to the wedding. Some pastors or counselors may find fewer sessions satisfactory, while others may wish to meet more often. As you use the premarriage inventory, you will find it adaptable to your particular style of counseling.

Obviously, not every question mentioned needs to be covered in the presence of the pastor or counselor. Six counseling sessions would not be enough to cover all the material in this inventory. Certain key questions may be covered, or the counseling session could revolve around problem questions which the couple encountered prior to meeting with the pastor or counselor. Use those questions that would be most beneficial to the couple you may be counseling.

Here is a suggested breakdown of the material for six counseling sessions.

PRIOR TO THE FIRST COUNSELING SESSION
—Assign chapters 1, 2, and 3 to be completed

SESSION I
—Discuss material in chapters 1, 2, and 3
—Assign chapters 4 and 5 as homework for Session II

SESSION II
—Discuss material in chapters 4 and 5
—Assign chapter 6 as homework for Session III

SESSION III
—Discuss material in chapter 6
—Assign chapter 7 as homework for Session IV

SESSION IV
—Discuss material in chapter 7
—Assign chapter 8 as homework for Session V

SESSION V
   —Discuss material in chapter 8
   —Assign chapters 9 and 10 as homework for
   Session VI

SESSION VI
   —Discuss material in chapters 9 and 10
   —Tie together any loose ends.

Additional Resources

   Chapters 11, 12, 13, 14, and 15 have been included as additional resource material. These chapters may or may not be used according to the needs of the couple and the counseling time that is available. [1]
   I feel that I must say a word about the material in the Sexual Inventory. In this chapter I have been very frank. The questions may be too embarrassing for some pastors, counselors or couples to discuss together. (I hope that this is not the case.) If the pastor or counselor does not feel comfortable in discussing some of these issues with the couple, may I suggest that they encourage the couple to discuss them together or with a doctor. These questions have been collected from counseling sessions with married couples, who have all expressed the wish that they had faced these issues prior to their marriage.

FOR TEACHERS AND LEADERS

   Teachers and leaders may wish to use this inventory as:

---

1. For additional help in premarital counseling I would suggest H. Norman Wright's book entitled **Premarital Counseling**, Moody Press.

—A course outline for teaching marriage and family issues.
—A source of communication questions for small groups in churches, homes, conferences or retreats.

FOR COUPLES ALONE

This inventory can be used with great benefit by couples who do not have the opportunity of premarital counsel with a pastor or counselor. The couple may use this as a guide to discussion in order to increase their communication with and knowledge of each other.

Married couples will find it helpful as a means to strengthen their relationship. They may also want to give this premarriage inventory as a gift to engaged couples they know.

1

Family

Background

"You're just like your mother!" "You act the same way your father does!" These common statements are heard time and time again. In many respects, we are a product of our environment for our family backgrounds do affect our lives.

The way our parents treated us many times affects the way we will treat our spouse. Family traditions or the lack of traditions will influence our future marriage. The social and financial status of our childhood years plays an important part in our adult thinking.

How much do you know about the family background of your future marriage partner? Are there potential problem areas? It has been said that when you marry, you marry the family. How well do you know your fiancé's family? Are you accepted by them? How well do they know you?

Answer the following questions and then discuss them together. Your discussion may trigger other family background questions which will, hopefully, help you gain a deeper insight into each other and your families.

1. How old were your parents when you were born?

Father _____   Mother _____

2. List your brothers and sisters in order of birth and include yourself:

    1. _____ Age ____ 4. _____ Age ____

    2. _____ Age ____ 5. _____ Age ____

    3. _____ Age ____ 6. _____ Age ____

3. Were your parents ever: ( ) Separated

    ( ) Divorced ( ) Widowed?

    How old were you at the time? _____

    My parents' divorce affected me by: _____

    _____

    _____

    _____

    _____

    Who raised you? ( ) Father ( ) Mother

    Other _____

4. My parents are still living: ( ) Yes ( ) No

5. My parents' occupations are:

    Father _____

Mother _____

6. I would describe my parents' marriage as:

   ( ) Very poor ( ) Sometimes troubled ( ) Middle-of-the-road ( ) Usually happy ( ) Very happy

7. I feel the leader in my home was:

   ( ) Father ( ) Mother ( ) Neither ( ) They fought for leadership.

8. Describe your relationship with your:

Father	*Mother*
( ) Affectionate	( ) Affectionate
( ) Accepted	( ) Accepted
( ) Tolerated	( ) Tolerated
( ) Rejected	( ) Rejected
( ) Persecuted	( ) Persecuted
( ) Other _____	( ) Other _____

   _____   _____

   _____   _____

9. Describe the discipline of your:

Father	*Mother*
( ) Domineering	( ) Domineering
( ) Strict	( ) Strict
( ) Firm but kindly	( ) Firm but kindly
( ) Permissive	( ) Permissive

( ) Indulgent   ( ) Indulgent

( ) Other _____ ( ) Other _____

_____ _____

_____ _____

10. I would describe my childhood as:

( ) Very poor ( ) Sometimes troubled ( ) Middle-of-the-road ( ) Usually happy ( ) Very happy ( ) Other _____

_____

_____

11. My parents think my marriage is: _____

_____

_____

_____

12. My parents' opinions towards my fiancé are:

_____

_____

_____

13. Regarding my marriage, the parents of my fiancé think that: _____

_____

_____

_____

14. The type of relationship I have with the parents of my fiancé is : _____

_____

_____

15. I see the following potential trouble points with my inlaws : _____

_____

_____

_____

_____

16. When I encounter difficulties with my in-laws, I will :

_____

_____

_____

_____

_____

17. I think the following traditions and family traits of my family will affect my marriage: _____

_____

_____

_____

_____

_____

18. After my marriage, if we live in the same house with my in-laws, I will: _____

_____

_____

_____

_____

_____

19. When my in-laws give advice, I will: _____

_____

_____

_____

_____

_____

20. I have the following questions about in-laws:

_____

_____

_____

_____

_____

_____

2

Previous
Marital History

You may have been married before. If so, please answer these questions. If you have not been married before please skip these questions and go on to the next chapter.

Many times, the individuals involved in second marriages carry into their new relationship problems and expectations out of their previous marriage. For example, if you had difficulty in communicating with your mate in your first marriage, will this trend continue? Why should your new relationship be any different? How will it be different. What will you do differently?

Problem areas are easier to identify than expectations. In your first marriage your mate may have taken care of and babied you when you were sick. In your second marriage, your mate may not baby you when you are sick. How will you feel about this? How will your new mate know what your expectations are?

The following questions are not exhaustive but may be helpful in starting discussion on potential problems and expectations brought about by more than one marriage.

1. Date of my first marriage : _____

2. How old were you and your spouse when you married?

   Myself _____   My spouse _____

3. How did the first marriage terminate?

   ( ) Divorce ( ) Annulment ( ) Death

4. My marriage lasted for _____ years.

5. Did you have any children by this marriage?

   ( ) Yes ( ) No

   Boys _____ Ages _____

   Girls _____ Ages _____

6. The strong points of this marriage were:

   A. _____

   B. _____

   C. _____

   D. _____

   E. _____

7. The conflict areas of this marriage were:

   A. _____

   B. _____

   C. _____

   D. _____

   E. _____

8. I have the following expectations about my new marriage, brought about by my previous marriage:

_____

_____

_____

_____

_____

If you have only had one previous marriage please skip these questions and go on to the next chapter.

1. Date of second marriage: _____

2. How old were you and your spouse when you married?

     Myself_____   My Spouse_____

3. How did the second marriage terminate?

     (   ) Divorce (   ) Annulment (   ) Death

4. My second marriage lasted _____ years.

5. Did you have any children by this second marriage?

     (   ) Yes (   ) No

   Boys _____ Ages_____

   Girls_____ Ages_____

6. The strong points of this marriage were:

   A. _____

   B. _____

C. _____

D. _____

E. _____

7. The conflict areas of this marriage were:

A. _____

B. _____

C. _____

D. _____

E. _____

8. I have the following expectations about my new marriage, brought about by my previous marriages:

_____

_____

_____

_____

_____

3

Status of
Present Relationship

Would you buy a car without shopping around? Would you purchase a house by only looking at the outside? Would you choose a vocation without looking at its positive and negative aspects? In most of the important decisions we usually shop around, weigh the advantages and disadvantages and count the cost. However, when it comes to one of the most important decisions in life—marriage—few people really examine the relationship to see if it is based on a solid foundation. How compatible are you with your future marriage partner? Do you have the same goals, interests and expectations? Could you see yourself living with that person for the rest of your life?

Answer the following questions and share together how you view your potential marriage partner.

1. I have known my fiancé for: _____

2. I first met my fiancé: _____

   _____

3. Have you announced your engagement yet?
   (   ) Yes (   ) No   (   ) Planning to on _____
   If yes, have you set a date for the wedding?

   _____

4. My fiancé and I see each other:
   (   ) Every day (   ) 1-2 Days per week (   ) 3-4 Days per week (   ) 5-6 Days per week (   ) Less than once a week, _____ per month.

5. Have you ever been engaged to anyone else?
   (   ) Yes (   ) No   How long ago? _____

6. The strong points that I see in my fiancé are:
   A. _____
   B. _____
   C. _____
   D. _____
   E. _____
   F. _____
   G. _____

7. I want to get married because: _____

   _____

   _____

   _____

8. My definition of love is:

   _____

   _____

   _____

_____

_____

9. My fiancé and I have the following interests in common:

_____

_____

_____

_____

_____

_____

10. I think a good sense of humor in marriage is important because:_____

_____

_____

11. I feel that my fiancé's manners are: _____

_____

_____

_____

12. My fiancé irritates me most when: _____

_____

_____

_____

13. I feel that our relationship has been most successful in:

_____

_____

_____

_____

14. I have the following expectations for my fiancé: (example: leader, good cook, gentle, provider, etc.)

A. _____

B. _____

C. _____

D. _____

E. _____

F. _____

G. _____

15. My fiancé has the following expectations for me:

A. _____

B. _____

C. _____

D. _____

E. _____

F. _____

G. _____

16. I am happiest in our relationship when: _____

_____

_____

_____

17. In our relationship I hurt most when: _____

_____

_____

_____

18. My fiancé and I differ about the following things:

A. _____

B. _____

C. _____

D. _____

E. _____

F. _____

19. The following are some of the goals that I would like to work toward in our marriage:

    A. _____

    B. _____

    C. _____

    D. _____

    E. _____

    F. _____

20. I believe my friends have the following opinions about this marriage: _____

    _____

    _____

    _____

    _____

21. Please check any of the following items which you feel could be a potential barrier to this marriage:

    (   ) Divorce

    (   ) Pregnancy

    (   ) Abortion

    (   ) Cultural differences

    (   ) Racial differences

(   ) Intellectual differences
(   ) Economic differences
(   ) Wide age difference
(   ) Young or early marriage
(   ) Parental conflicts
(   ) Sexual problems
(   ) Homosexual background
(   ) Physical handicaps
(   ) Personality differences

Explain each item you checked:

_____

_____

_____

_____

_____

_____

_____

_____

_____

_____

_____

4

Religious Background

Most people want a church wedding rather than a civil ceremony. Have you ever wondered why? What is so special about a church wedding? Sometimes the couple really want their marriage blessed of God while others want a church wedding simply because it is a tradition. How important are religious and spiritual values to a marriage relationship? Does the spiritual life of the couple affect their marriage? Do the vows of commitment made before God and friends really mean anything?

Answer the following questions and share with one another your religious and spiritual convictions.

1. My father's religious background is:

   _____

2. How religious is your father?

   ( ) Very ( ) Middle-of-the-road ( ) Not very
   ( ) Not at all

3. My mother's religious background is:

   _____

4. How religious is your mother?

   ( ) Very ( ) Middle-of-the-road ( ) Not very
   ( ) Not at all

5. My religious background is:

   _____

6. How important do you believe religious commit-
   ments are to your marriage?

   _____

   _____

   _____

   _____

7. Do you believe in God? ( ) Yes ( ) No
   ( ) Unsure

8. Do you pray? ( ) No ( ) Once in a while
   ( ) Very often

9. Do you read the Bible? ( ) No ( ) Occasionally
   ( ) Fairly regularly ( ) Regularly

10. Do you and your fiancé read the Bible together?
    ( ) Yes   ( ) No

    If yes, how often do you read together?_____

    _____

11. Do you and your fiancé pray together? ( ) Yes
    ( ) No
    If yes, how often do you pray together?_____

    _____

12. I attend the services of a church: (   ) Never
    (   ) Seldom (   ) Periodically (   )Frequently
    (   ) Regularly

13. I attend: _____ church.
    Are you a member? (   ) Yes   (   ) No

14. What do you think it means to receive Christ as
    your Savior and Lord? _____

    _____

    _____

    _____

    _____

15. Have you ever personally received Christ as your
    Savior and Lord?
    (   ) Yes (   ) No (   ) Unsure   If yes, where?

    _____

    When? _____

16. What do you think it means to be a Spirit-filled
    Christian?

    _____

    _____

    _____

    _____

17. Do you consider yourself to be a Spirit-filled Christian?　( ) Yes ( ) No ( ) Don't know

18. My most significant spiritual experience was:

_____

_____

_____

_____

_____

19. My definition of a Christian marriage is:

_____

_____

_____

_____

20. I want a church wedding because:

_____

_____

_____

_____

_____

21. A Christian marriage is important to me because:

   _____

   _____

   _____

   _____

22. Do you believe that it is important for you and your family to go to church?   ( ) Yes   ( ) No
   ( ) Unsure   Explain: _____

   _____

   _____

   _____

   _____

23. We plan to go to _____ church after we are married.

24. My fiancé and I have the following religious differences: _____

   _____

   _____

   _____

   _____

25. My fiancé and I plan to work on our religious differences by : _____

   _____

   _____

   _____

   _____

   _____

26. To me, equality before God means : _____

   _____

   _____

   _____

   _____

27. I believe that spiritual leadership in the home is initiated by : _____

   _____

   _____

   _____

   _____

28. I think that the spiritual growth of my children is the responsibility of : _____

_____

_____

_____

_____

29. We are planning for the following type of family devotions: _____

_____

_____

_____

_____

_____

30. What do you think the phrase "To marry in the Lord" means? _____

_____

_____

_____

31. Read Ephesians 5:15-6:4; Colossians 3:21; I Timothy 5:8; I Peter 3:7, and make a list of the responsibilities of a Christian husband. _____

_____

_____

_____

_____

_____

_____

_____

32. Read Ephesians 5:15-6:4; I Timothy 1:9-10, 3:11; I Peter 3:1-6, and make a list of the responsibilities of a Christian wife. _____

_____

_____

_____

_____

_____

33. I think that Psalm 127:1 means:

_____

_____

_____

34. To me the word submission in Ephesians 5:21-22 means:

   _____

   _____

   _____

   _____

35. Does only the wife submit?   ( ) Yes ( ) No
   ( ) Uncertain

36. I feel a husband can submit in marriage by:

   _____

   _____

   _____

   _____

   _____

37. After reading Genesis 2:24, I feel the phrase "one flesh" means: _____

   _____

   _____

   _____

   _____

38. Read Deuteronomy 24:1-4; Malachi 2:11-16; Matthew 5:31-32; 19:3-12; Mark 10:2-12; Luke 16:18; and I Corinthians 7:10-15. After reading the above scriptures, I feel God's attitude toward divorce is:

_____

_____

_____

_____

39. I have the following questions about spiritual matters:

_____

_____

_____

_____

_____

_____

5

Children

In many premarital counseling programs the issue of child rearing is not dealt with in great detail. This is usually because of a time factor, and because most couples are more concerned with immediate issues such as finances, marriage plans and the sexual side of marriage.

Some couples do not plan for children or use forms of birth control. Others can't wait to have children. What are your thoughts? Do you feel you should have children right away or do you plan to get to know your marriage partner better before having children? How long should a couple wait?

The questions listed below are designed to help you formulate your thoughts and verbally set forth a plan for child rearing. Share together your thinking in this important area of marriage.

1. Do you plan to have children?   ( ) Yes ( ) No
   ( ) Undecided

2. How many children would you like to have?_____

3. How long would you like to wait before having

   children? _____

4. Should a couple wait until they can afford to have children?   ( ) Yes   ( ) No   ( ) Undecided

5. I feel that it is important for the father to be present at the birth of a child. ( ) Yes ( ) No ( ) Undecided

6. If we cannot have children, my feelings about adoption are: _____

_____

_____

_____

7. What are your feelings if you would have only boys or only girls?

_____

_____

_____

_____

8. How much should a husband participate in the care of a baby? _____

_____

_____

_____

9. What are your feelings toward sharing equally in all of the activities of care and raising of children?

(feeding, changing of diapers, late night responsibilities, etc.) _____

_____

_____

_____

10. The names of children should be determined by:

_____

_____

11. The responsibility for the discipline of the children lies with: ( ) Husband   ( ) Wife   ( ) Both

12. I want my children to learn the following values, rules and characteristics: _____

_____

_____

_____

_____

_____

13. My parents used the following discipline with me:

14. I will want to discipline my children in the following ways:

Early years _____

_____

_____

_____

Middle years _____

_____

_____

Teen years _____

_____

_____

15. Who should be responsible for assisting children with homework?   (   ) Husband (   ) Wife (   ) Both

16. My thoughts with regard to leaving children with baby-sitters are:

_____

_____

_____

_____

_____

17. Who is responsible for buying clothes for the children?   ( ) Husband   ( ) Wife   ( ) Both

    Comments: _____

    _____

    _____

    _____

18. Who decides what gifts to buy for the children?
    ( ) Husband   ( ) Wife   ( ) Both

19. I feel that the place of pets in the home is:

    _____

    _____

    _____

    _____

20. I feel that favoritism of children in the home is:

    _____

    _____

    _____

    _____

21. What is your opinion about standing behind your mates' discipline of the children? _____

_____

_____

_____

_____

22. If you have children by a previous marriage, what will you want the relationship to be with the new father/mother? _____

_____

_____

_____

23. If you have children by a former marriage, who will discipline your children? _____

_____

_____

_____

_____

24. If you have children by a former marriage, do you foresee any problems with visiting rights of the divorced partner? Explain:

_____

_____

_____

25. In discipline, how strict do you think parents should be?

_____

_____

_____

_____

26. I think the most important thing in child discipline is:

_____

_____

_____

_____

27. I think that praising your children involves: _____

_____

_____

_____

_____

28. How much should parents sacrifice for their children?

_____

_____

_____

_____

29. What are your thoughts about parents caring more for the children than for each other? _____

_____

_____

_____

_____

30. I think that children should have the following privileges:

Early years _____

_____

_____

Middle years _____

_____

_____

Teen years _____

_____

_____

31. What message do you think is conveyed in Psalm 127 and Psalm 128? _____

_____

_____

_____

32. Read Proverbs 22:6; 22:15; 13:24; 23:13-14; 29:15; 19:18; 29:17; Hebrews 12:5-11; Proverbs 20:30; Ephesians 6:4. After reading these verses, I think that God's attitude toward discipline is: _____

_____

_____

_____

_____

_____

_____

33. I think that having children will teach me the following lessons: _____

_____

_____

_____

_____

_____

34. I have the following questions concerning child rearing: _____

_____

_____

_____

_____

_____

6

Finances

Every couple experiences some degree of conflict or frustration in the area of finances. Next to communication and sex, finances rate among the big three of marital problems. The vast majority of couples who go into divorce courts are head over heals in debt.

How do you handle finances? Are you a spender or a saver? Do you like to use charge cards? Do you have a budget? Robert J. Hastings thinks that, "money management is not so much a technique as it is attitude. And when we talk about attitudes, we are dealing with emotions. Thus, money management is basically self-management or control of one's emotions. Unless one learns to control himself, he is no more likely to control his money than he is to discipline his habits, his time or his temper. Undisciplined money usually spells undisciplined persons."[1] Do you agree with Mr. Hastings?

Fill out the following questions and share with your fiancé your thoughts concerning finances.

1. Robert J. Hastings, **The "10-70-20" Formula for Wealth: From the Marriage Affair** [Wheaton, Illinois: Tyndale House Publishers, 1971), p. 363.

1. My attitude about the wife working outside the home is:

   _____

   _____

   _____

   _____

2. State your attitude about the wife working outside the home after the birth of children: _____

   _____

   _____

   _____

   _____

3. Are you going to pool financial resources? (gifts, savings and earnings) Explain: _____

   _____

   _____

   _____

   _____

4. If you have been married before, do you have any reservations or do you feel that there will be any problems in pooling finances from the former

marriage? (gifts, properties, savings, investments, insurance, trust funds or wills, etc.) Explain:_____

_____

_____

_____

_____

_____

5. I foresee the following problems with the "my money, your money" feelings:_____

_____

_____

_____

6. My attitude toward debt, credit cards, borrowing money and buying on time is:_____

_____

_____

_____

_____

7. When we experience financial reverses (unemployment, debt, sickness, etc.) I plan to:

_____

_____

_____

_____

_____

8. Who will handle the checkbook? _____

_____

9. Who will pay the bills? _____

_____

10. What is your plan for budgeting?

_____

_____

_____

_____

_____

_____

_____

11. How generous are you? _____

_____

_____

12. What are your thoughts about giving? (church, charities, etc.). _____

_____

_____

_____

13. What are your thoughts about saving money? (savings accounts, investments, property, retirement) _____

_____

_____

_____

_____

_____

14. What are your thoughts about life insurance?_____

_____

_____

_____

_____

15. What are your thoughts about health insurance?

_____

_____

_____

_____

16. How do you feel about writing a will?

_____

_____

_____

17. What are your thoughts about the possibility of someday being financially responsible for your in-laws?

_____

_____

_____

_____

18. How do you feel about the husband holding extra or part-time jobs? _____

_____

_____

_____

19. What financial aspects do you think are involved in entertaining guests in your home? _____

_____

_____

_____

20. When we get into financial difficulties I will:

_____

_____

_____

_____

21. I have the following questions about finances:

_____

_____

_____

_____

_____

_____

_____

_____

_____

SUPER SIMPLE BUDGET

A Super Simple Budget has been included for those couples who do not have a system of budgeting finances. There are usually three problem areas in family finances:

First, most couples do not know what the total of their fixed monthly expenses are (line 5). Because of this they buy items and have no idea of where they are financially until they are out of funds. (Very few arguments occur over fixed monthly expenses. You pay the rent or you are out on your ear. You pay your gas and electricity or they are turned off . . . without any argument.)

The second problem area occurs when the couple has bills totaling more than their monthly controllable income (line 6). When this happens the couple usually puts all of their controllable monies on their bills. This eliminates any extra cash flow. With no cash flow the couple can become frustrated and hostile. They have no money for an emergency, entertainment, or medicine.

The couple might be wise to set aside some money for emergencies that may arise.

The third problem area revolves around who pays the bills. If one mate is not aware of how their money is being spent there can be trouble. For those who pay the bills I suggest the following:

1. Pay the fixed monthly expenses (usually no argument).

2. Come to your mate with the total of the fixed monthly expenses and the total of miscellaneous expenses. Show them what needs to be paid and how much you have to pay with.

3. Ask them which bills they think need to be paid first and how much should be put on each bill. Then pay the bills as you both agreed.

4. When your mate then asks you why a certain bill has not been paid you can relate to them your discussion and that you paid the bills according to your agreement.

THE SUPER SIMPLE BUDGET

INCOME (Monthly)

1. Salary or wages—Husband ("take-home" after deductions) $ _____
2. Salary or wages—Wife ("take-home" after deductions) $ _____
3. Other income (only list regular monthly income) $ _____
4. TOTAL CASH—("take-home" income per month) $ _____

FIXED MONTHLY EXPENSES

A. Giving $ _____   *TITHING*—Means giving 10% of all income.

B. House payment/rent $ _____

C. Gas & Electricity $ _____

D. Water & Garbage $ _____   *LOVE GIVING*—Means giving out of love and in response to the benefits received from the Lord.

E. Food & Household items $ _____

F. Car payment $ _____   *FAITH GIVING*—Means a promise to give an amount beyond ordinary income.

G. Gasoline & Oil $ _____

H. Car Insurance $ _____

I. Life Insurance $ _____   *SACRIFICE GIVING*—Means giving to the Lord something which I really needed and wanted.

J. Loans $ _____

K. Union dues $ _____

L. Phone $ _____   EVERYONE MUST MAKE UP HIS OWN MIND AS TO HOW MUCH HE SHOULD GIVE. II

M. _____ $ _____   Corinthians 9:7, TLB

N. _____ $ _____

5. TOTAL FIXED EXPENSES $ _____   *****   Enter Total Cash from Line 4 and subtract Line 5

TOTAL CASH LINE (4) $ _____

FIXED EXPENSES (5) $ _____

6. TOTAL FLEXIBLE OR CONTROLLABLE MONIES LESS FIXED EXPENSES $ _____

MISCELLANEOUS EXPENSES TO BE PAID FROM MONIES ON LINE SIX

A. Doctor, Dentist, Drugs
B. Clothing
C. Gifts
D. Entertainment, Recreation

E. Allowances
F. Education, Lessons
G. Savings (Some place their savings in Fixed Monthly Expenses)

H. Car maintenance
I. Charge accounts
J. Babysitting
K. Home improvements
L. Subscriptions
M. Appliances
N. Incidentals

Controllable monies from
Line 6 $ _____

Less BUFFER OR EMER- *
GENCY MONIES $ _____

TOTAL $ _____

WHO PAYS THE BILLS? *

7

Communication

Reuel Howe, a gifted communicator feels that, "dialogue is to love, what blood is to the body. When the flow of blood stops, the body dies. When dialogue stops, love dies and resentment and hate are born. But dialogue can restore a dead relationship. Indeed, this is the miracle of dialogue: it can bring relationship into being, and it can bring into being once again a relationship that has died."[1]

Marjorie Umphrey in her book *Getting To Know You* defines communication as the following:

1. Communication is giving and receiving a message.

2. Communication is giving of oneself.

3. Communication is receiving part of someone else.

4. Communication is sharing ideas, feelings and moments with another person.

5. Communication is experiencing another human being.

---

1. Reuel L. Howe, **The Miracle of Dialogue**, (New York: The Seabury Press, 1963), p. 3.

6. Communication is the giving and receiving of an emotional stroke.

7. Communication is getting my needs met.

8. Communication is meeting another person's needs.

9. Communication is looking at and seeing what another person is saying.

10. Communication is listening and hearing what others are saying.

11. Communication is my face and body talking.

12. Communication is using all my senses to recognize what the other's face and body and voice is saying.

13. Communication is putting myself in the other's place.

14. Communication is touching.

15. Communication is reaching out.

16. Communication is tenderness and caressing.

17. Communication is words on the printed page.

18. Communication is allowing someone else to intrude into your world of thoughts.

19. Communication is expression through the arts.

20. Communication is spiritual. [2]

How well are you communicating? How open are you with each other? Do you feel free enough for your

2. Marjorie Umphrey, **Getting To Know You** (Irvine, California: Harvest House Publishers, 1976), pp. 20-21.

future life partner to get to know the real you? Answer the following questions and explore with your fiancé your deeper thoughts and feeling.

1. I think a person can change their mate by: _____

_____

_____

_____

_____

2. When I am emotionally irritated or bothered, my tendency is to: ( ) act out or come on strong .
( ) withdraw and go into quiet irritation

3. State your opinion about keeping each other informed regarding schedules and whereabouts:

_____

_____

4. What will you do when your companion continually refers to your faults? _____

_____

_____

_____

_____

5. List things you think you would talk about at mealtimes:

_____

_____

_____

_____

6. How much should you share with your partner about work and other interests? _____

_____

_____

_____

_____

7. I can become more aware of my mate's feelings by:

_____

_____

_____

_____

8. How much time should be devoted to leisure time activities? _____

_____

_____

_____

9. How much time should be devoted to the family?

_____

_____

_____

_____

10. How much time should be devoted to former friends?

_____

_____

_____

_____

11. When I find my mate remaining silent for a long period of time, I will: _____

_____

_____

_____

12. To what extent do you think your mate should pursue his/her interests, activities and sports?

_____

_____

_____

_____

13. When I find that my mate is not as affectionate as I would like, I will: _____

_____

_____

_____

14. When my mate yells at me, I will: _____

_____

_____

_____

_____

15. I think I can lift the spirits of my mate when he/she is depressed or discouraged by: _____

_____

_____

_____

_____

16. When you have a major illness strike your mate
    how will you react? _____

    _____

    _____

    _____

17. When my mate does something that displeases me,
    I will:

    _____

    _____

    _____

    _____

18. You may love your mate but what are your
    thoughts about him/her being your friend? _____

    _____

    _____

    _____

    _____

19. When my mate sulks, whines or pouts, I will:

_____

_____

_____

_____

20. When I find that my mate is not listening to me, I will:

_____

_____

_____

_____

21. When my mate uses the phrases "You always," "You never," or "Everytime," I will respond by:

_____

_____

_____

_____

22. What are your thoughts about sharing unpleasant things that happen during the day? _____

_____

_____

_____

_____

23. I think I can help develop my mate's self-image by:

_____

_____

_____

24. In clarifying misunderstood statements, I will:

_____

_____

_____

25. I think that my mate and I need to improve our communication in the following areas: _____

_____

_____

_____

_____

26. I think that my mate would like to change the following qualities or behaviors in me: _____

_____

_____

_____

_____

27. I express love to my mate in the following ways:

_____

_____

_____

_____

28. What are your feelings about marriage counselors and pastors helping you to solve personal and marital problems? _____

_____

_____

_____

29. I have the following educational plans: _____

_____

_____

_____

_____

30. I have the following vocational plans: _____

_____

_____

_____

_____

31. I would like to ask the following questions about
communication in marriage: _____

_____

_____

_____

_____

_____

_____

_____

_____

_____

ADDITIONAL COMMUNICATION QUESTIONS FOR DISCUSSION

1. I think that the best time of day to talk over marital difficulties is:

2. The types of things that get on my nerves are:

3. State your opinion about your partner talking about former sweethearts or a former spouse:

4. When my mate says one thing and means another, I will:

5. I can compliment and praise my spouse more by:

6. When my mate goes out often with the guys/girls, I feel:

7. What are your thoughts about telling jokes at your partner's expense?

8. What are your opinions about correcting your mate in public?

9. I like to do the following activities with my mate:

10. When I find it difficult to confide in my mate, I will:

11. How can you help your mate when he/she is upset because of work, children or some conflict with another person outside of your marriage? How much sympathy do you give? How much encouragement? How much correction?

12. What is your opinion about discussing your spouse's faults in public?

13. What are your thoughts about non-verbal communication in marriage?

14. What are your thoughts about arguing in public?

15. It has been said that marriage is a fifty-fifty partnership. What do you think?

16. I am easily offended in the following ways:

17. What are your thoughts about discussing in-laws in public?

18. I think that personality clashes are caused by:

19. I think that jealousy and possessiveness are caused by:

20. How important do you think it is for a husband and wife to discuss intellectual and emotional issues like race relations, politics, religion, etc.?

8

Sexual Inventory

Seldom does a week go by that I don't do some form of sexual counseling. I never cease to be amazed, that although we live in a sex-saturated culture, little good sex knowledge is known by the common man or woman on the street. I have had individuals in the office who stated that their families were very open in the discussion of sex. Also, that they felt they were very knowledgeable in this area. Yet, as we talked further I could see how little they knew and how embarrassed they were to talk on this subject.

The following questions are frank and deal with common problems encountered in giving sexual counsel. It has been my experience that most couples do not talk about sexual matters very deeply, even after they are married. These questions deal with real issues. A great deal of frustration, hurt, fear and anger could be eliminated if these issues were faced by the couple before they became crisis points in what is designed by God to be a most beautiful experience.

May I encourage you to discuss together the following questions.

1. Have you had a physical examination for your marriage?   (   ) Yes   (   ) No

2. Do you have any health problems? Explain: _____

_____

_____

_____

_____

3. At this particular time, I think about sex? ( ) Seldom ( ) Periodically ( ) Frequently ( ) Regularly

4. My present feelings about sex are: ( ) Disturbed ( ) Fearful ( ) Anxious ( ) Neutral ( ) Expectant ( ) Excited ( ) Intrigued

5. Do you have any sexual inhibitions, fears or awkward feelings? Explain: _____

_____

_____

_____

_____

_____

6. What was your impression of your parents' sex life? ( ) Fulfilling ( ) Warm ( ) Casual ( ) Neutral ( ) Tolerant ( ) Cold ( ) Empty

7. Were you the victim of any unpleasant sexual experience as a child, adolescent or adult? ( ) No
( ) Indecent exposure ( ) Homosexual
( ) Molested ( ) Raped ( ) Incest

Other _____

8. Who do you think is responsible for birth control?
( ) Husband   ( ) Wife   ( ) Both

9. In planning to postpone having children, the form of birth control method I prefer is ( ) Withdrawal
( ) Rhythm( ) Douche( ) Foam( ) Vaginal suppositories ( ) Contraceptive jelly ( ) Condom
( ) Diaphragm( ) Cervical Cap( ) IUD( ) Birth control pills ( ) Vasectomy ( ) Hysterectomy
( ) Abortion

10. Who do you think should initiate sexual activity?

_____

Why? _____

_____

_____

_____

11. Who do you think should determine the way, the place, how often, length of time and variety of sexual activity?

_____

_____

_____

12. How do you feel about seeing your partner nude?

    _____

13. How do you feel about having your partner seeing you nude? _____

    _____

14. State your thoughts about the following:

    Lip kissing _____

    Tongue kissing _____

    Your partner kissing your body_____

    _____

    Kissing of your partner's body _____

    _____

    Caressing your partner's body_____

    _____

    Your partner caressing your body_____

Kissing of your partner's genitals _____

Your partner kissing your genitals _____

Bringing your partner to a climax by hand _____

Your partner bringing you to a climax by hand ____:

Bringing your partner to a climax by oral stimulation _____

Your partner bringing you to a climax by oral
stimulation _____

15. How important do you think simultaneous orgasm
is?_____

16. A woman reaches orgasm by : _____
   _____
   _____
   _____
   _____

17. Why is it important to communicate about sexual desires?

   _____

   _____

   _____

   _____

18. Why is it important to verbally tell your partner what stimulates you sexually? _____

   _____

   _____

   _____

   _____

19. What are your thoughts about intercourse during the wife's menstrual period? _____

   _____

_____

_____

_____

20. What type of menstrual period do you/does your fiancé have? _____

_____

_____

_____

21. How many times per week do you think that you would like to have intercourse? _____

22. I think the act of intercourse should last: _____

_____

_____

23. I would prefer a lovemaking environment that includes (lighting, music, etc.): _____

_____

_____

_____

_____

_____

24. Privacy in lovemaking is important because:

_____

_____

_____

_____

25. At what time of day should lovemaking take place?

_____

26. What are your thoughts as to where lovemaking should take place? _____

_____

_____

_____

27. What are your thoughts about various positions in intercourse? _____

_____

_____

28. What will you do when you find the man has difficulty in maintaining an erection?

_____

_____

_____

_____

29. What will you do when you find the man has difficulty with premature ejaculation? _____

_____

_____

_____

30. What will you do when you find the woman cannot reach a climax? _____

_____

_____

31. What will you do when you find the woman cannot reach a climax with the penis inserted into the vagina?

_____

_____

_____

_____

_____

32. How important do you think the act of intercourse is on the Honeymoon night? _____

_____

_____

_____

_____

33. What will you do when you find that the husband cannot make entrance into his wife and complete the act of intercourse due to tightened vaginal muscles or pain in the vaginal area? _____

_____

_____

_____

34. Suppose that you have been married for a period of time, and one day you discover your mate masterbating. What will you do? _____

_____

_____

_____

_____

35. Tell what you might do when you find that your partner does not like the act of intercourse? _____

_____

_____

_____

_____

36. How do men and women differ in their readiness for sexual climax? _____

_____

_____

_____

_____

37. If and when I discovered my partner was romantically interested in another person, I would: _____

_____

_____

_____

_____

_____

38. Why are things like kind words, gentle touch and kind deeds important in the lovemaking process?

_____

_____

_____

39. Do you think that you will be able to refuse sexual requests of your partner without offending him/her? ( ) Yes ( ) No ( ) Uncertain

What will you say? _____

_____

_____

_____

40. How much bathroom privacy do you feel is needed?_____

_____

_____

_____

_____

41. I have a lack of sexual knowledge in the following
    areas:

    _____

    _____

    _____

    _____

    _____

    _____

42. How tense are you as you answer these questions?

    _____

    _____

    _____

43. Do you believe in counseling for sexual problems?
    (   ) Yes (   ) No (   ) Uncertain

44. Who would you feel free to talk with concerning
    sexual problems? _____

    _____

45. After reading I Corinthians 6:15-20 and I Thessa-

lonians 4:1-8, state what you think is God's view of premarital intercourse: _____

_____

_____

_____

46. In Hebrews 13:4 it says, "Marriage should be honored by all, and the marriage bed kept pure." I think this means: _____

_____

_____

_____

_____

_____

47. After reading I Corinthians 7:3-5, the concept I think the writer is trying to convey is: _____

_____

_____

_____

_____

_____

48. I have the following questions about sexual matters:

_____

_____

_____

_____

_____

_____

_____

_____

RESOURCES

THE ACT OF MARRIAGE by Tim and Beverly LaHaye

This book contains valuable information on all aspects of sex from a Christian viewpoint.

"The art of mutually enjoyable lovemaking is not difficult to learn, but neither is it automatic. No one is a good lover by nature . . . Yet no one need settle for a lifetime of sexual frustration."

Thus Tim and Beverly LaHaye sum up this book—a most practical, thorough, and useful Christian handbook on sexual love.*.

*The above resources may be ordered from:

FAMILY SERVICES
P.O. Box 124
Fresno, California 93707

SEX AND THE COMMITTED CHRISTIAN by Ken Poure

A six tape cassette album on "what you've always wanted to know about sex but were afraid to ask your pastor." As the father of three, Ken also draws witty and informative illustrations on rearing children from his storehouse of experience.

Tape Titles:

Husband and Wife Relationships (for wives only)
Husband and Wife Relationships (for husbands only)
Dare to Discipline
Development of Character
The Other Side of Sex
Life Styles*

*The above resources may be ordered from:

FAMILY SERVICES
P.O. Box 124
Fresno, California 93707

9
Sample
Wedding Ceremony

Introduction by Minister

_____Bill_____ and ____Susan____, you are surrounded by your family and friends, all of whom are here to share in your joy on this special occasion. It will be one of the most memorable and happy days of your lives.

On this your wedding day, you stand apart from all other beings. You stand within the beautiful circle of your love. For this reason we are here in the presence of God, to join you both in holy marriage. God has declared that marriage is an honorable and desirable state. It was designed by God to bring the ultimate in happiness and personal satisfaction. The basic guidelines are that you should put God first, the welfare of your mate second and yourself last.

Minister speaks to both sets of parents

Would Mr. and Mrs. __Johnson__ and Mr. and Mrs. ____Wilson____ please stand. It is traditional for the father of the bride to give her away. However, in a real sense, both sets of parents share in the giving and receiving. Therefore, Mr. and Mrs. Johnson , do you not only give your son   Bill   to be Susan's husband, but also joyfully receive Susan as your daughter? (Response by parents—"We do.") Mr. and Mrs. Wilson , do you not only joyfully give your daughter Susan to Bill as his wife, but receive Bill to be your son? (Response by parents—"We do.")

Bride and Groom
move to Altar

Minister proceeds   Marriage was instituted by God Himself when He said, "It is not good that man should be alone."

From the side of man God created woman to be his friend and companion . . .

—Not out of his head to rule over him.

—Not out of his feet to be trampled upon by him

—But out of his side to be equal with him

—And under his arm for protection

—And near his heart to be loved.

God said, "For this cause shall a man leave father and mother, and shall cleave to his wife, and they two shall be one flesh."

—One flesh in companionship

—One flesh in the control of the God given sexual drives

—One flesh in the propagation of children

—And one flesh in the testimony of the joy of a Christian marriage.

The Bible's description of true love

The Bible tells us that true love is "slow to lose patience . . . love is kind . . . love looks for a way of being constructive. Love is not possessive . . . love is neither anxious to impress nor does it cherish inflated ideas of its own importance.

"Love has good manners and does not pursue selfish advantage. Love is not touchy. Love does not keep account of evil or gloat over the wickedness of other people. On the contrary, love is glad with all good men when truth prevails.

"Love knows no limit to its endurance, no end to its trust, no fading of its hope; love can outlast anything. Love is, in fact, the one thing that still stands when all else has fallen." I Corinthians 13

Admonition of Scripture to husbands and wives

In the book of Ephesians, chapter five, marriage is likened to the mystical union of Christ and the church . . .

"You wives must submit to your husbands' leadership in the same way you submit to the Lord. For a husband is in charge of his wife in the same way Christ is in charge of his body the church. (He gave his very life to take care of it and be its savior!) So you wives must willingly obey your husbands in everything, just as the church obeys Christ.

The minister may possibly want to make personal comments to the Bride at this point

"And you husbands, show the same kind of love to your wives as Christ showed to the church when he died for her.

"That is how husbands should treat their wives, loving them as parts of themselves. For since a man and his wife are now one, a man is really doing himself a favor and loving himself when he loves his wife! No one hates his own body but lovingly cares for it, just as Christ cares for his body the church, of which we are parts.

The minister may possibly want to make personal comments to the Groom at this point

"So again I say, a man must love his wife as part of himself; and the wife must see to it that she deeply respects her husband . . . obeying . . . praising and honoring him."

Vows spoken to the Minister

After hearing the admonition of Scripture, do you＿＿Bill＿＿take ＿＿Susan＿＿to be your lawfully wedded wife? Do you promise to support her and love her for life? Do you solemnly pledge before God and these witnesses that you will be faithful to her for the remainder of your life? If so, answer, I will. (Response by the Groom)

＿＿Susan＿＿do you take＿Bill＿ to be your lawfully wedded husband? Do you promise to love, honor and obey him? Do you solemnly pledge before God and these witnesses that you will be his faithful wife until you are separated by death? If so, answer, I will. (Response by the Bride)

Minister will have the Bride pass her flowers to her Maid of Honor . . . Bride and Groom will turn and face each other and will hold hands

Minister proceeds
with personal
vows

_____Bill_____ please repeat after me: I love you____Susan____, and today in the presence of our families and friends, I pledge myself to you. I reaffirm my faith in Christ and dedicate our marriage to be Christ-centered. I promise before God to love you, to honor you and cherish you. As God enables me, I will provide for all your needs and desires.____Susan____, I love you . . . Be my wife.

____Susan____ please repeat after me:____Bill____, I love you. I've longed for this day . . . to be able to say publicly to our families and friends, that you are truly a man of God. A man that is tender and sensitive in his love for others. I promise, to make you a home where there is peace for your soul and joy for your heart. My goal is to be a Godly woman and to help fulfill our goals and dreams. I need you and I am proud to become your wife.

Exchange of
rings

What symbols do you offer that you will faithfully fulfill these promises? (Minister will collect the rings)

May the circle of this ring typify your unending happiness and love, and may the triangle formed in its passing, to me, and to one another, signify that triune relationship with God who reigns above where all true marriages are made. (Minister will hand back the rings to be placed on the Bride's finger and then on the Groom's.)

Bride and Groom will again turn toward each other and hold hands

Minister proceeds

Will you please both repeat after me: I give you this ring as a seal of my commitment and responsibility to you in the presence of these witnesses, in the name of the Father, Son and Holy Spirit.

Since____Bill____and____Susan____ have consented together in these promises and have symbolized this by the giving and receiving of these rings, I now pronounce them husband and wife. Whom God has joined together, let no man dare to separate.

Minister will pray . . . Couple may be standing or kneeling . . . they may wish to light a Unity candle . . . after which they will again stand before the

Minister and face
each other, holding
hands

Ceremony of the
Unity Candle

The two outside candles of the center candelabra are lit to represent your lives to this moment. They are two distinct lights, each capable of going their separate ways. To bring bliss and happiness to your home, there must be the merging of these two lights into one light. This is what the Lord meant when He said, "On this account a man shall leave his father and mother and be joined to his wife and the two shall be one flesh."

From now on your thoughts shall be for each other rather than for your individual selves. Your plans shall be mutual, your joys and sorrows shall be shared alike.

As you each take a candle and together light the center one you will not extinguish your own candle as is usually done. Instead, place the outside candles back in their original places still lit symbolizing your individual personalities that remain, yet lives that merge together as one.

As the center candle is lit, may the radiance of this one light be a testimony of your unity in the Lord Jesus Christ.

Bride and Groom kiss

Minister proceeds It is my pleasure now to introduce to you for the first time Mr. and Mrs. _____ Johnson _____.

10

Wedding Checklist

Date of Wedding _____ Hour _____

Name of Church, Building or Home _____

Address _____

City _____ Phone _____

IN CONTACTING A CHURCH FOR YOUR WEDDING YOU MAY WISH TO KNOW:

( ) Procedure for reserving the facilities.

( ) Whether or not the church has a Wedding Hostess.

( ) Policies concerning marrying those who have been divorced, mixed religion and whether marriages are permitted on Sunday.

( ) Policies concerning premarital counseling.

( ) Cost, which would include use of facilities, Wedding Hostess and janitorial clean up.

( ) Whether or not the church has reception facilities.

( ) Special rules or restrictions concerning photography or decorations.

( ) Available facilities for the Bridal Party.

( ) Does the church provide equipment like a kneeling bench, candle holders or arches.

( ) Permission for soloists, choir or other special music.

( ) Other _____

_____

_____

If you are planning a non-traditional wedding in a park, forest, meadow, sea or lake shore or some other setting you will need to consider the following:

( ) Accessibility to those in your wedding party.

( ) Adequate parking.

( ) Privacy

( ) Will everyone be able to hear the ceremony? Sounds do not usually carry well out of doors.

( ) Alternate plans in case of bad weather

_____

_____

_____

CLERGYMAN OR PRESIDING OFFICIAL

Name _____ Phone _____
Sometimes more than one clergyman or official will take part in a wedding ceremony.

2nd Name _____ Phone _____

APPOINTMENT TO DISCUSS WEDDING

Date _____ Hour _____

Rehearsal Date _____ Hour _____

YOU MAY WISH TO DISCUSS:

( ) Honorarium $ _____

( ) Use of a second clergyman or official.

  Honorarium $ _____

( ) Any special vows you may wish to incorporate?

( ) Premarital counseling

  Date _____ Hour _____

  Date _____ Hour _____

  Date _____ Hour _____

  Date _____ Hour _____

  Date _____ Hour _____

  Date _____ Hour _____

WEDDING HOSTESS

Name _____ Phone _____

Special Arrangements _____
_____
_____

_____

_____

Honorarium $_____

FLORIST

Name _____

Address _____

Phone _____ Conference Date _____

YOU MAY WISH TO DISCUSS:
- ( ) Bride's Bouquet
- ( ) Bride's going away corsage
- ( ) Bouquets for Bride's attendants
- ( ) Corsages for mothers of the Bride and Groom
- ( ) Corsages for grandmothers
- ( ) Boutonnieres for Groom, ushers, fathers and clergyman
- ( ) Corsages for friends and/or relatives serving at the reception
- ( ) Church decorations and carpet
- ( ) Reception decorations
- ( ) Time and place of delivery _____

_____

- ( ) Special arrangements _____

_____

_____

_____

PHOTOGRAPHER

Name _____

Address _____

Phone _____ Conference Date _____

YOU MAY WISH TO DISCUSS:

( ) Types of pictures he takes—ask to see some of his finished work.

( ) The cost—get a firm price on pictures and albums.

( ) If he will take any special pictures you may request.

( ) When pictures will be taken—before, during or after the wedding.

( ) Expected delivery date of finished pictures.

( ) Special arrangements _____

_____

_____

_____

CATERER

Name _____

Address _____

Phone _____ Conference Date _____

YOU MAY WISH TO DISCUSS:
( ) Wedding cake
( ) Napkins
( ) Punch bowl
( ) Silver
( ) Beverages
( ) Menu _____

_____

_____

_____

_____

( ) If reception is out of doors, what is an alternate
plan in case of bad weather _____

_____

_____

( ) Special arrangements _____

_____

_____

_____

MUSIC

Organist

    Name _____ Phone _____

    Honorarium $ _____

Soloist

    Name _____ Phone _____

    Honorarium $ _____

Any other special music

    _____

    _____

    _____

Musical selections

    _____

    _____

    _____

    _____

    _____

Music at the reception

    Name_____ Phone _____

    Honorarium $_____

Musical selections

_____

_____

_____

_____

_____

INVITATIONS, ANNOUNCEMENTS
AND STATIONARY

_____ Number invited to ceremony

_____ Number invited to reception

_____ Number to receive announcements

( ) Date to be mailed _____

( ) Postage

( ) Thank you cards

( ) Printing expenses

( ) Name of printer _____

Address _____

Phone _____ Delivery Date _____

( ) Special arrangements _____

_____

_____

_____

_____

BRIDAL GOWN

Shop _____

Date for fitting _____

Delivery date _____

Special arrangements _____

_____

_____

BRIDESMAIDS GOWNS

_____

_____

_____

_____

_____

_____

ATTENDANTS

Maid of honor _____ Phone _____

    Dress size _____ Shoe _____ Gloves _____

Bridesmaid _____ Phone _____

    Dress size _____ Shoe _____ Gloves _____

Bridesmaid _____ Phone _____

    Dress size _____ Shoe _____ Gloves _____

Bridesmaid _____ Phone _____

    Dress size _____ Shoe _____ Gloves _____

Bridesmaid _____ Phone _____

    Dress size _____ Shoe _____ Gloves _____

Bridesmaid _____ Phone _____

    Dress size _____ Shoe _____ Gloves _____

Best Man _____ Phone _____

    Tuxedo size _____ Shoe _____

Groomsman _____ Phone _____

    Tuxedo size _____ Shoe _____

Groomsman _____ Phone _____

Tuxedo size _____ Shoe _____

Groomsman _____ Phone _____

Tuxedo size _____ Shoe _____

Groomsman _____ Phone _____

Tuxedo size _____ Shoe _____

Groomsman _____ Phone _____

Tuxedo size _____ Shoe _____

USHERS

Name _____ Phone _____

Name _____ Phone _____

Name _____ Phone _____

Name _____ Phone _____

Name _____ Phone _____

Name _____ Phone _____

FLOWER GIRL

Name _____ Phone _____

RING BEARER

Name _____ Phone _____

CANDLELIGHTERS

Name _____ Phone _____

Name _____ Phone _____

GIRLS AT GUESTBOOK

Name _____ Phone _____

Name _____ Phone _____

SERVERS AT RECEPTION

Name _____ Phone _____

Name _____ Phone _____

Name _____ Phone _____

Name _____ Phone _____

Name _____ Phone _____

Name _____ Phone _____

Name _____ Phone _____

Name _____ Phone _____

JANITOR

Name _____ Phone _____

SPECIAL PEOPLE

_____

_____

_____

_____

WEDDING GIFT LIST

FLATWARE PATTERN: ( ) Sterling ( ) Silver-
plate ( )Stainless( ) Other

Pattern _____ Registered at _____

Registered at _____

Registered at _____

DINNERWARE PATTERN: ( ) China ( ) Stone-
ware, Earthenware
( ) Other

Pattern _____ Registered at _____

Registered at _____

Registered at _____

GLASSWARE PATTERN: ( ) Crystal ( ) Glass
( ) Barware

Pattern _____ Registered at _____

Registered at _____

Registered at _____

OTHER ITEMS THAT MAY BE LISTED

( ) Linens

( ) Kitchen utensils

( ) Housewares and appliances

( ) Furniture and accessories

( ) Luggage

( ) Cleaning tools

MISCELLANEOUS ITEMS CHECKLIST

( ) Wedding rings—check engraving

( ) Marriage license

( ) Medical examination and blood tests

( ) Purchase of guest book

( ) Gifts for bridesmaids

( ) Gifts for groomsmen

( ) Honeymoon—reservations, tickets, car etc.

( ) Newspaper announcement

( ) Transportation for wedding party

( ) Arrange for out of town guests

( ) Appointment with hairdresser or barber

( ) Luggage for honeymoon

( ) Change Social Security card to married name

( ) Change driver's license to married name

( ) Change names on insurance policies

( ) Make out a will

( ) Make arrangements for tape recording the wedding ceremony

( ) Open checking and savings accounts in joint names

( ) Arrange a spinster dinner or a bachelor party

( ) Arrange for after-rehearsal dinner

( ) Something old, something new, something borrowed and something blue.

GUEST LIST

BRIDE'S RELATIVES

_____

_____

_____

_____

_____

_____

_____

_____

_____

_____

_____

_____

_____

_____

_____

_____

_____

_____

_____

_____

GUEST LIST

GROOM'S RELATIVES

_____

_____

_____

_____

_____

_____

_____

_____

_____

_____

_____

_____

_____

_____

_____

_____

_____

_____

_____

_____

_____

_____

_____

_____

GUEST LIST

FRIENDS

_____

_____

_____

_____

_____

_____

_____

_____

_____

_____

_____

_____

_____

_____

_____

Additional
Resources

11

Danger Signs

Marriage is a very important decision. We need to be sure we are making the right choice of a marriage partner. Anthony Florio, a professional marriage counselor, lists the following danger signs to look for:

Like red lights, blinking, danger signs mean STOP, then proceed with caution (if at all!) It is better to take this brief test before you become engaged so that if definite danger signs turn up you will have time to do something about them before committing yourself officially to marriage plans. If you are already engaged and encounter danger signs, then by all means delay your wedding plans until you can straighten out the problem areas that you or your partner have. Like icebergs, the negative traits may be hidden from you, and just the tips show what is going on beneath a supposedly mature exterior.

1. *A general uneasy feeling about the relationship. Lack of inner peace.* A nagging, aching, disturbing inside that says, "Something is wrong." Don't ignore that feeling. It may be your own temporarily numbed common sense, or it may be God's Spirit trying to communicate something to you. More than a few clients have admitted to me that they knew the marriage was a mistake even as they were walking down the aisle.

2. *Frequent arguments.* Never sure how the date will end. More fighting than fun.

3. *Avoiding discussing sensitive subjects because you're afraid of hurting your partner's feelings* or starting an argument. You find yourself thinking, "I'd better not talk about this." Perhaps subjects like: "I wish he'd show me more affection, I wish he wouldn't treat his mother so mean. I wonder why he always has a temper tantrum when he gets a flat. Can't he control it better? I wish he would shower more often."

"She makes a pig of herself when there's a box of candy anywhere in sight—don't you suppose she cares about getting fat? I wish she'd read a book once in a while. Why can't we ever talk about something interesting instead of just superficial topics?

4. Getting more involved physically. You resolve to limit the acceleration of your physical intimacy, but find that on each new date you start again at the place where you left off. Sometimes couples get involved physically as a way to avoid arguments. Just one of the reasons for this being a danger sign is that your relationship may remain on the physical level only, throughout your courtship and marriage. After you're married you may not like the personality that goes along with the body.

5. If you find yourself always doing what your partner wants you to do. Constantly giving in, being accommodating. This could indicate a

selfish, domineering partner and/or a serious insecurity on your part.

6. If you detect serious emotional disturbances such as extreme fears, extreme shyness, bizarre behavior, irrational anger, inflicting physical injury, inability to demonstrate affection.

7. If you feel you are staying in the relationship through fear. For example, if thoughts like these go through your mind: "I wish I could get out of dating him, but I'm afraid of what he might do to me. Or he might commit suicide. I feel trapped and I couldn't stand the guilt if something happened."

8. If your partner is constantly complaining about apparently unreal aches and pains and going from doctor to doctor.

9. If your partner continually makes excuses for not finding a job. If he or she borrows money from you frequently. The partner who evades responsibility and who can't manage his money wisely will be a poor marriage risk.

10. If your partner is overly jealous, suspicious, questions your word all the time, feels that everyone is against him.

11. If the one you date is a perfectionist and is constantly critical. This kind of person often creates a tense unhealthy atmosphere.

12. Treats you contemptuously. Uses biting sarcasm.

13. Parents and other significant people are strongly against your marriage. Consider their reasons before you make a final decision.

14. Lack of spiritual harmony.

15. Few areas of common interest.

16. Inability to accept constructive criticism. Doesn't apologize when he is wrong.

DANGER SIGNS THAT WOULD INDICATE THE NEED FOR PROFESSIONAL COUNSELING

1. Undue jealousy, suspicion, distrust.

2. Constant chip-on-the-shoulder attitude.

3. Temper tantrums.

4. Unresolved anger, resentment. Vindictiveness.

5. Physically abusive.

6. Objects to or is distant to any kind of romantic involvement.

7. Severe mood swings. High elation followed by depression.

8. Constantly negative attitude. Pessimistic.

9. Suspicious of everyone. Suspects some sort of plotting against him.

10. Speaks of suicide and the meaninglessness of
    life.[1]

1. From **Two To Get Ready**, Fleming H. Revell Company, 1974. Used by
permission.

12

Discerning Genuine Love

"I love to eat." "I love to swim." "I love money." "I love my dog." "I love you." What does the word *love* mean? Webster defines love as: "1. A feeling of strong personal attachment induced by sympathetic understanding, or by ties of kinship; ardent affection. 2. Tender and passionate affection for one of the opposite sex."

There are different types of love: Love of things, self love, brotherly love, sexual love and Godly love. How does the love you feel for your fiancé compare with God's definition of love as found in I Corinthians chapter thirteen?

Take this short test and compare your love and the love of your fiance with the Biblical definition of love.

Rate yourself and your fiancé on a scale of one to ten. One would be low on the love scale and ten would be high. Circle the number which you believe is descriptive of you and your fiancé at this time.

Example: *This love of which I speak is: Slow to lose patience*

Myself   1 ②3 4 5 6 7 8 9 10

Fiancé   1 2 3 4 5 6 7 8 ⑨ 10

By circling "two," you would be saying that you do

not have a great deal of patience. On the other hand, your fiancé displays a great deal of patience as noted by circling the number "nine."

1. *This love of which I speak is: Slow to lose patience*

   Love doesn't demonstrate irritations or reflect anger or have a quick temper. Love bears ill treatment from others. Love has fully accepted the character of the other individual. Love is long suffering.

   Myself 1 2 3 4 5 6 7 8 9 10

   Fiancé 1 2 3 4 5 6 7 8 9 10

2. *Love looks for a way of being constructive*

   Love is actively creative. Love is able to recognize needs. Love mellows all which would be harsh and austere. Love discovers successful methods of improving or contributing to the other's life.

   Myself 1 2 3 4 5 6 7 8 9 10

   Fiancé 1 2 3 4 5 6 7 8 9 10

3. *Love is not possessive*

   Love is not envious. Love does not hold exclusive control where one is allowed little or no freedom to fulfill himself apart from the other individual. Love does not boil over with jealousy.

   Myself 1 2 3 4 5 6 7 8 9 10

   Fiancé 1 2 3 4 5 6 7 8 9 10

4. *Love is neither anxious to impress*

   Love does not brag. Love doesn't seek to make an

impression or create an image for personal gain. Love does not show itself off. Love is not ostentatious. Love does not make a parade.

Myself   1 2 3 4 5 6 7 8 9 10
Fiancé   1 2 3 4 5 6 7 8 9 10

5. *Nor does love cherish inflated ideas of its own importance*

Love does not put on airs. Love is not self-centered. Love has the ability to change and to accept change. Love is flexible. Love is not conceited, arrogant and inflated with pride. Love doesn't allow or accept life to revolve around itself. Love is not on an ego trip.

Myself   1 2 3 4 5 6 7 8 9 10
Fiancé   1 2 3 4 5 6 7 8 9 10

6. *Love has good manners*

Love has respect for others which results in a set of Christ-centered standards. Love does not act unbecomingly or unmannerly. Love has discretion and knows what is proper and when. Love is not indecent.

Myself   1 2 3 4 5 6 7 8 9 10
Fiancé   1 2 3 4 5 6 7 8 9 10

7. *Love does not pursue selfish advantage*

Love does not insist on its own way. Love does not have primary concern for personal sexual appetites or social status but concern for needs of the other person and other family members. Love does not pursue selfish aims.

Myself 1 2 3 4 5 6 7 8 9 10
Fiancé 1 2 3 4 5 6 7 8 9 10

8. *Love is not touchy*

Love is not easily angered. Love is not hypersensitive or easily hurt. Love does not take things too personally. Love is thick skinned. Love is not emotionally involved with personal opinions so that to reject ideas is to reject the one giving them. Love bears no malice. Love is not irritable or resentful.

Myself 1 2 3 4 5 6 7 8 9 10
Fiancé 1 2 3 4 5 6 7 8 9 10

9. *Love does not keep account of evil*

Love doesn't review wrongs which have been forgiven. Love doesn't dwell on past evil. Love keeps no score of past hurts. Love destroys evidence of past mistakes when possible

Myself 1 2 3 4 5 6 7 8 9 10
Fiancé 1 2 3 4 5 6 7 8 9 10

10. *Love does not gloat over the wickedness of other people*

Love doesn't compare self with others for self-justification. Love doesn't use other's evil to excuse personal weakness. Love doesn't say, "Everyone's doing it." Love does not rejoice at injustice and unrighteousness.

Myself 1 2 3 4 5 6 7 8 9 10
Fiancé 1 2 3 4 5 6 7 8 9 10

11. *On the contrary, love is glad with all godly men when truth prevails*

    Love is active in fellowship with dedicated Christians. Love is occupied with spiritual objectives. Love rejoices at the victory of truth.

    Myself   1 2 3 4 5 6 7 8 9 10
    Fiancé   1 2 3 4 5 6 7 8 9 10

12. *Love knows no limit to its forbearance*

    Love has the ability to live with the inconsistencies of others. Love is slow to expose. Love can overlook faults. Love has empathy for the problems of others. Love can endure many hardships.

    Myself   1 2 3 4 5 6 7 8 9 10
    Fiancé   1 2 3 4 5 6 7 8 9 10

13. *Love knows no end to its trust*

    Love expresses faith in everything. Love believes in the person and the person's worth without question. Love is eager to believe the best and has no reason to doubt the person's integrity.

    Myself   1 2 3 4 5 6 7 8 9 10
    Fiancé   1 2 3 4 5 6 7 8 9 10

14. *Love knows no fading of its hope*

    Love is not fickle. Love has perfect peace and confidence that God is primarily responsible for introducing the right partner at the right time. Love is positive and not negative.

Myself   1 2 3 4 5 6 7 8 9 10
Fiancé   1 2 3 4 5 6 7 8 9 10

15. *Love has unlimited endurance*

Love is able to outlast anything. Love is able to endure all obstacles and even love in the face of unreturned love. Love does not lose heart but has perseverance. There is nothing that love cannot face.

Myself   1 2 3 4 5 6 7 8 9 10
Fiancé   1 2 3 4 5 6 7 8 9 10

If you love someone you will be loyal to him no matter what the cost. You will always believe in him, always expect the best of him, and always stand your ground in defending him.

Love is the one thing that still stands when all else has fallen.

In this life we have three great lasting qualities . . . Faith, Hope and Love. But the greatest of them is Love.

Love is not just a feeling but a commitment of the person and his or her will. Love is a decision to love an imperfect person.

13

Descriptive Characteristics

Place an X by each word which you *honestly believe* is descriptive of you or your fiancé. Then discuss your findings with each other. Explain the reason why you chose a particular word.

	Myself	*My Fiancé*
1. Persuasive	———	———
2. Wonderful	———	———
3. Peaceful	———	———
4. Enthusiastic	———	———
5. Boisterous	———	———
6. Soothing	———	———
7. Magnetic	———	———
8. Forceful	———	———
9. Friendly	———	———
10. Unselfish	———	———
11. Timid	———	———
12. Tolerant	———	———
13. Brave	———	———
14. Slow	———	———
15. Proud	———	———
16. Exciting	———	———
17. Attractive	———	———
18. Deliberate	———	———

19. Confident _____ _____
20. Open-minded _____ _____
21. Generous _____ _____
22. Bitter _____ _____
23. Calm _____ _____
24. Outgoing _____ _____
25. Shy _____ _____
26. Patient _____ _____
27. Self-motivated _____ _____
28. Compassionate _____ _____
29. Talented _____ _____
30. Kind _____ _____
31. Ambitious _____ _____
32. Softhearted _____ _____
33. Gifted _____ _____
34. Egotist _____ _____
35. High-spirited _____ _____
36. Happy _____ _____
37. Humble _____ _____
38. Undisciplined _____ _____
39. Shallow _____ _____
40. Spiritually mature _____ _____
41. Bad mouth _____ _____
42. Suspicious _____ _____
43. Overbearing _____ _____
44. Touchy _____ _____
45. Jealous _____ _____
46. Gossip _____ _____
47. Nervy _____ _____
48. Magnificent _____ _____
49. Stubborn _____ _____
50. Big-hearted _____ _____
51. Cautious _____ _____
52. Stimulating _____ _____
53. Afraid _____ _____

54. Outspoken _____ _____
55. Helpful _____ _____
56. Materialistic _____ _____
57. Unhealthy _____ _____
58. Insensitive _____ _____
59. Gentle _____ _____
60. Humorous _____ _____
61. Unattractive _____ _____
62. Competent _____ _____
63. Daring _____ _____
64. Religious _____ _____
65. Dynamic _____ _____
66. Well-mannered _____ _____
67. Superior _____ _____
68. Stern _____ _____
69. Venturesome _____ _____
70. Faithful _____ _____
71. Conceited _____ _____
72. Selfish _____ _____
73. Polite _____ _____
74. Eager _____ _____
75. Hostile _____ _____
76. Aggressive _____ _____
77. Disrespectful _____ _____
78. Wishy-washy _____ _____
79. Dishonest _____ _____
80. Moody _____ _____
81. Dependable _____ _____
82. Overly competitive _____ _____
83. Talkative _____ _____
84. Weak-willed _____ _____
85. Personable _____ _____
86. Strong-willed _____ _____
87. Angry _____ _____
88. Productive _____ _____

89. Gifted   _____   _____
90. Negative   _____   _____
91. Idealistic   _____   _____
92. Impractical   _____   _____
93. Easy-going   _____   _____
94. Stingy   _____   _____
95. Conservative   _____   _____
96. Loud   _____   _____
97. Independent   _____   _____
98. Sarcastic   _____   _____
99. Decisive   _____   _____
100. Self-sufficient   _____   _____
101. Analytical   _____   _____
102. Theoretical   _____   _____
103. Loyal   _____   _____
104. Unsociable   _____   _____
105. Calm   _____   _____
106. Apprehensive   _____   _____
107. Diplomat   _____   _____
108. Unmotivated   _____   _____
109. Restless   _____   _____
110. Exaggerates   _____   _____
111. Optimistic   _____   _____
112. Domineering   _____   _____
113. Leader   _____   _____
114. Unemotional   _____   _____
115. Sensitive   _____   _____
116. Self-sacrificing   _____   _____
117. Critical   _____   _____
118. Dependable   _____   _____
119. Indecisive   _____   _____
120. Warm   _____   _____
121. Undependable   _____   _____
122. Carefree   _____   _____
123. Fearful   _____   _____

124. Practical   _____   _____
125. Inconsiderate   _____   _____
126. Confident   _____   _____
127. Crafty   _____   _____
128. Perfectionist   _____   _____
129. Rigid   _____   _____
130. Revengeful   _____   _____
131. Efficient   _____   _____
132. Spectator   _____   _____
133. Sensible   _____   _____
134. Self-protective   _____   _____
135. Independent   _____   _____

14

Insight Questions

Please complete the following sentences. From your answers you will gain new insight into your thoughts and feelings.

1. When I hear from others that you have complained about me I _____
   _____

2. When some other interest seems more important to you than I do, I _____
   _____

3. When you seem to hold back something from me, I _____

4. When I hold back something from you, I _____

5. When you look at other men/women with obvious interest, I _____
   _____
   _____

6. When you are late and I have to wait for you, I _____
   _____

7. When you have a strong interest which I cannot share, I _____
_____

8. When I try to convince you of something and you can't accept it, I _____

9. When you seem to be rejecting my feelings, I _____
_____

10. When you praise or compliment me, I _____
_____

11. When I am confronted with or think of that which I fear most, I _____
_____

12. When I think you are judging me, I _____
_____

13. When you become violently angry with me, I _____
_____

14. When I have to admit that I am wrong, I _____
_____

15. When I think you are taking a superior role in our dialogues and discussions, I _____
_____

16. When I do not seem able to reach you, I _____
_____

17. When you frown at me, I _____
_____

18. When you are being too hard on yourself, I _____
_____

19. When you smile at me, I _____
_____

20. When you reach out and touch me, I _____

21. When I think of praying with you, I _____
_____

22. When you make a sacrifice for me, I _____
_____

23. When others notice our closeness, I _____
_____

24. When we appear as a partnership, not as individuals only, I _____
_____

25. When I reflect that you love me, I _____
_____

26. When you seem annoyed with me, I _____
_____

27. When I have the opportunity to be alone and enjoy some solitude, I _____
_____

28. When we have been separated a long time, I _____
_____

29. When I reflect that we are growing in mutual knowledge, I _____
_____

30. When we are holding hands, I _____
_____

31. When we are making plans together, I _____

32. When I am buying you a gift, I _____
_____

33. When I reach out and touch you, I _____
_____

34. When you interrupt me in conversation, I_____
_____

35. When we are in some form of competition like cards

    or an athletic contest, I _____
_____

36. When you say "no" to one of my requests, I _____
_____

37. When I think I have hurt your feelings, I _____
_____

38. When you apologize to me, I _____
_____

39. When we can spend a quiet evening together, I ____
_____

40. When you help me locate my feelings, I _____
_____

41. When I hear from others that you have "bragged"

    about me, I _____

42. When others look at you with obvious interest, I __
_____

43. When you cry, I _____
_____

44. When you are sick, I _____
_____

45. When I think about your death and what life will be without you, I _____

46. When we hear "our song," I _____

47. When you ask me to help you, I _____

48. When I have to apologize to you, I _____

49. When you surprise me with something nice, I _____

50. When you seem to appreciate me, I _____

51. When you laugh at my jokes, I _____

52. When I think that you are not recognizing my needs, I _____

53. When I make a mistake and you point it out, I _____

54. When you are holding me in your arms, I _____

55. When our routines are different and our interests separate us, I _____

56. When I am late and you have to wait for me, I _____

57. When I reach out to touch you, I _____
_____

58. When I think you don't believe me, I _____
_____

These Insight Questions are reprinted from *The Secret of Staying in Love* by John Powell. Used by permission from Argus Communications, Niles, Illinois.

15

Decisions in Marriage

There are many decisions that have to be made in a marriage. Some are made by the husband, some are made by the wife and some are shared equally. Read over the following list of decisions and indicate who you feel should make the decision. (H for husbands . . . W for wives . . . B for both.) then compare your answers with the answers of your fiancé.

1. Who decides on formal or informal engagement? _____
2. Who decides date of wedding? _____
3. Who decides what type of wedding? _____
4. Who decides whether to have a honeymoon? _____
5. Who decides where to go on a honeymoon? _____
6. Who decides where to live? _____
7. Who decides when to move? _____
8. Who decides whether the wife should work? _____
9. Who decides whether the wife should give up her job when a child is born? _____
10. Who decides financial decisions? _____
11. Who decides if incomes are to be shared? _____
12. Who decides who will handle the checkbook? _____
13. Who decides about borrowing money and going into debt? _____
14. Who decides on the budget? _____

15. Who makes justified complaints to tradesmen? ___
16. Who decides to buy a car? ___
17. Whose name is the car in? ___
18. Who looks after the car? ___
19. Who decides which house to buy? ___
20. Whose name is it in? ___
21. Who decides on the interior decor? ___
22. Who decides on the exterior decor? ___
23. Who decides on the furnishings? ___
24. Who decides on the landscaping? ___
25. Who takes care of the yard work? ___
26. Who is responsible for life and health insurance? ___
27. Who makes retirement plans? ___
28. Who decides activities after retirement? ___
29. Who takes the active role in sex? ___
30. Who decides whether to have children? ___
31. Who takes responsibility for contraception? ___
32. Who decides when to have children? ___
33. Who decides how many children to have? ___
34. Who takes responsibility for the education of the children? ___
35. Who takes responsibility in emergencies? ___
36. Who helps with the homework? ___
37. Who decides political issues for the family? ___

38. Who decides which premarriage friends to socialize with? ___
39. Who invites people to the house? ___
40. Who chooses television programs? ___
41. Whose food tastes prevail? ___
42. Who plans the day-by-day meals? ___
43. Who does the grocery shopping for the family? ___

44. Who decides when to go out?　　　　　——
45. Who decides where to go out?　　　　　——
46. Who decides what to do and where to go on vacations?　　　　　——
47. With whose relatives do you keep in touch?　——
48. Whose job is it to keep in touch with the relatives?　　　　　——
49. Who remembers anniversaries and birthdays?　　　　　——
50. Who copes with family disasters?　　　——
51. Who decides whether to go to church or not?——
52. Who decides which church to go to?　　——

SUGGESTED READING LIST

A GUIDE TO CHILD REARING
  By Dr. Bruce Narramore, Zondervan, 1972.

AN OUNCE OF PREVENTION
  By Dr. Bruce Narramore, Zondervan, 1973.

ARE YOU FUN TO LIVE WITH?
  By Lionel Whiston, Word Books, 1968.

BEFORE YOU MARRY
  By Petersen and Smith, Tyndale House, 1974.

BEING A MAN IN A WOMAN'S WORLD
  By James Kilgore, Harvest House, 1975

BUDGETS, BEDROOMS, AND BOREDOM
  By E. Russell Chandler, Regal Books, 1976

CARING ENOUGH TO CONFRONT
  By David Augsburger, Regal Books, 1974

CHERISHABLE LOVE AND MARRIAGE
  By David W. Augsburger, Herald Press, 1973

CHRISTIAN LIVING IN THE HOME
  By Jay E. Adams, Baker Books, 1974

CONFIDENT CHILDREN
  By Richard Strauss, Tyndale House, 1975

DISCOVERING THE INTIMATE MARRIAGE
  By R.C. Sproul, Bethany Fellowship, 1975

DO YOURSELF A FAVOR: LOVE YOUR WIFE.
  By Page Williams, Logos Books, 1973

FOREVER MY LOVE
  By Margaret Hardisty, Harvest House, 1975.

FULFILLED MARRIAGE
  By Norman Wright, Harvest House, 1976.

GAMES HUSBANDS AND WIVES PLAY
  By John W. Drakeford, Broadman Press, 1970

GETTING MORE FAMILY OUT OF YOUR DOLLAR
  By James Kilgore, Harvest House, 1976.

GETTING TO KNOW YOU
  By Marjorie Umphrey, Harvest House, 1976.

GOOD TIMES FOR YOUR FAMILY
By Wayne E. Rickerson, Regal Books, 1976.

HAPPINESS IS A FAMILY TIME TOGETHER
By Lois Bock and Miji Working, Fleming H. Revell, 1975.

HEAVEN HELP THE HOME
By Howard Hendricks, Victor Books, 1973.

HELP I'M A PARENT
By Dr. Bruce Narramore, Zondervan, 1971.

HOW TO BE HAPPY THOUGH MARRIED
By Tim La Haye, Tyndale House, 1968.

HOW TO DEVELOP YOUR CHILD'S TEMPERAMENT
By Beverly La Haye, Harvest House, 1977.

HOW TO SUCCEED WITH YOUR MONEY
By George Bowman, Moody Press, 1974.

I AM A MOTHER
By Ella May Miller, Spire Books, 1976.

I WANT MY MARRIAGE TO BE BETTER
By Henry Brandt and Phil Landrum, Zondervan, 1976.

INTENDED FOR PLEASURE (Tapes also available)
By Ed Wheat and Gaye Wheat, Fleming H. Revell Co., 1977.

IT'S ALL IN THE FAMILY
By Ken Poure, Accent Books, 1975.

I WANT TO ENJOY MY CHILDREN
By Dr. Henry Brandt and Phil Landrum, Zondervan, 1975.

LETTERS TO KAREN
By Charlie W. Shedd, Spire Books, 1965.

LETTERS TO PHILIP
By Charlie W. Shedd, Spire Books, 1969.

MAGNIFICENT MARRIAGE
By Gordon MacDonald, Tyndale House, 1976.

MAKE MORE OF YOUR MARRIAGE
By Gary R. Collins, Word Books, 1976.

MARRIAGE IS FOR LOVE
By Richard Strauss, Tyndale House, 1973.

MAXIMUM MARRIAGE
By Tim Timmons, Fleming H. Revell, 1976.

SEX FOR CHRISTIANS
By Lewis B. Smedes, Eerdmans Publishing, 1976.

SEXUAL HAPPINESS IN MARRIAGE
By Herbert J. Miles, Zondervan, 1967.

SEXUAL MATURITY FOR WOMEN
By Mary Deatrick, Vision House, 1976.

SMART DADS I KNOW
By Charlie W. Shedd, Sheed and Ward, Inc., 1975.

STRAW HOUSES IN THE WIND
By C.C. Carlson, Harvest House, 1974.

TALK TO ME
By Charlie W. Shedd, Doubleday and Company, 1975.

THE ACT OF MARRIAGE
By Tim and Beverly La Haye, Zondervan, 1976.

THE CHRISTIAN FAMILY
By Larry Christenson, Bethany Fellowship, 1970.

THE FAMILY FIRST
By Kenneth O. Gangel, His Internal Service, 1972.

THE FULFILLED WOMAN
By Lou Beardsley and Toni Spry, Harvest House, 1975.

THE HAPPY HOME HANDBOOK
By Jo Berry, Fleming H. Revell, 1976.

THE INTIMATE MARRIAGE
By Clinebell and Clinebell, Harper and Row, 1970.

THE MARRIAGE AFFAIR
By J. Allen Petersen, Tyndale House, 1971.

THE SECRET OF STAYING IN LOVE
By John Powell, Argus Communications, 1974.

THE SPIRIT-CONTROLLED WOMAN
By Beveraly La Haye, Harvest House, 1976.

TRAIN UP A CHILD
By Richard D. Dobbins, Baker Book House, 1973.

THOROUGHLY MARRIED
  By Dennis Guernsey, Word Books, 1975.

TWO TO GET READY
  By Anthony Florio, Fleming H. Revell, 1974.

WHAT IS A FAMILY
  By Edith Schaeffer, Fleming H. Revell, 1975.

WHAT KIDS KATCH FROM PARENTS
  By Norma Steven, Harvest House, 1976.

WHAT WIVES WISH THEIR HUSBANDS KNEW ABOUT WOMEN
  By Dr. James Dodson, Tyndale House, 1975.

WHY AM I AFRAID TO TELL YOU WHO I AM?
  By John Powell, Argus Communications, 1969.

YOU CAN BE A GREAT PARENT
  By Charlie Shedd, Word Books, 1976.

YOU CAN HAVE A HAPPIER FAMILY
  By Norm Wakefield, Regal Books, 1977.

YOU CAN WIN WITH LOVE
  By Dale E. Galloway, Harvest House, 1976.

YOUR FINANCES IN CHANGING TIMES
  By Larry Burkett, Campus Crusade, 1975.

NOTES, COMMENTS, INSIGHTS

OTHER GOOD BOOKS FROM HARVEST HOUSE

HOMEMAKING, An Invitation to Greatness, Norma Steven and Joyce Orwick. Recently a young mother of four wrote to Norma for help in her role as a homemaker. Through their letters Norma shares housekeeping hints, recipes and thoughts from the Word. It is the authors' prayer that you will catch a glimpse of the homemaker's high calling and find your invitation to greatness. 1156—$2.95 (paper)

FOREVER MY LOVE, Margaret Hardisty, writes from a woman's point of view of the husband's responsibility to his wife, his family and his church. She explains the female mind in a way that allows the husband to provide for the *emotional* needs of his wife. This outspoken book, appealing to husband and wife alike, is the first of its kind for today's man. 0117—$2.95 (paper)

GETTING TO KNOW YOU, A Guide to Communicating. Meaningful relationships established on a healthy one-to-one basis through the neglected ways of communication is the central theme of this unique book by Dr. Marjorie Umphrey. Helps are offered on breaking down barriers of communication—with your spouse, your peers and your children. 0257—$2.95 (paper)

BEFORE YOU SAY "I DO," Wes Roberts and H. Norman Wright. This study manual, a creative resource for premarital preparation and enrichment, is designed to assist you as you prepare for one of the most significant experiences of your life. Couples committed to making their marriage a fulfilling and growing relationship will find a wealth of practical ideas for building a firm foundation for their future together. 1199—$2.95 (paper) This manual can also be used as an ideal companion to the cassette series BEFORE YOU SAY "I DO." 1288—$26.95

LETTERS ON LIFE AND LOVE. Dr. James Kilgore, a Christian Psychologist, shares personal letters from women that have been received and answered by him regarding the problem areas of life and love. Dr. Kilgore deals honestly and openly with some of the very touchy personal questions that women want to know about, but are often afraid to ask. This small book should be very helpful to thousands of women. 1121—$1.75 (mass)

WHAT KIDS KATCH FROM PARENTS. This warm-hearted mother-to-mother look at the role of mother-hood, and the enjoyable rigors of raising a family, shows that children can be trained "in the way they should go." Norma Steven tells of her feeling and experiences throughout twenty-two years of mother-hood—of how kids KATCH more than they are taught. A delightful book for every parent. 0222—$1.60 (mass)

 Harvest House Publishers
2861 McGaw
Irvine, CA 92714